Use this page to record your baby's footprints

3 months

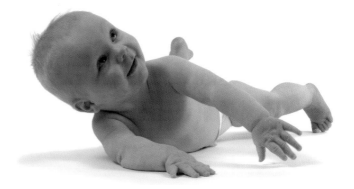

First U.S. edition 2006

ISBN 0-7636-3091-8

10 9 8 7 6 5 4 3 2 1

Printed in Hong Kong

This book was typeset in Eureka Sans & Braganza.
The photographs were taken using a Fuji S2
digital camera fitted with a 60mm micro Nikkor lens,
lit by Elinchrom flash, then processed using
Apple computers running Adobe software.

Photographer's assistant: Rebecca Fairbairn
Models & styling by Caroline Repchuk
Designed by Mike Jolley and edited by Sue Harris, The Templar Company plc

First published in the United States and Canada by Candlewick Press
2067 Massachusetts Avenue
Cambridge, Massachusetts 02140

visit us at www.candlewick.com

David Ellwand

b unique moments
y

a record book

Candlewick Press
Cambridge, Massachusetts

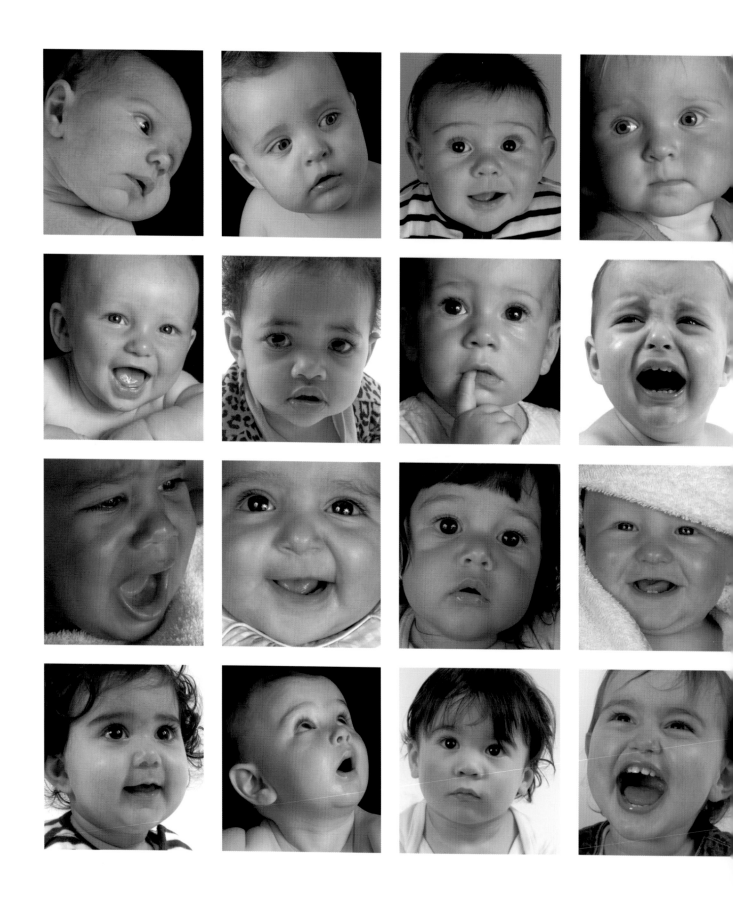

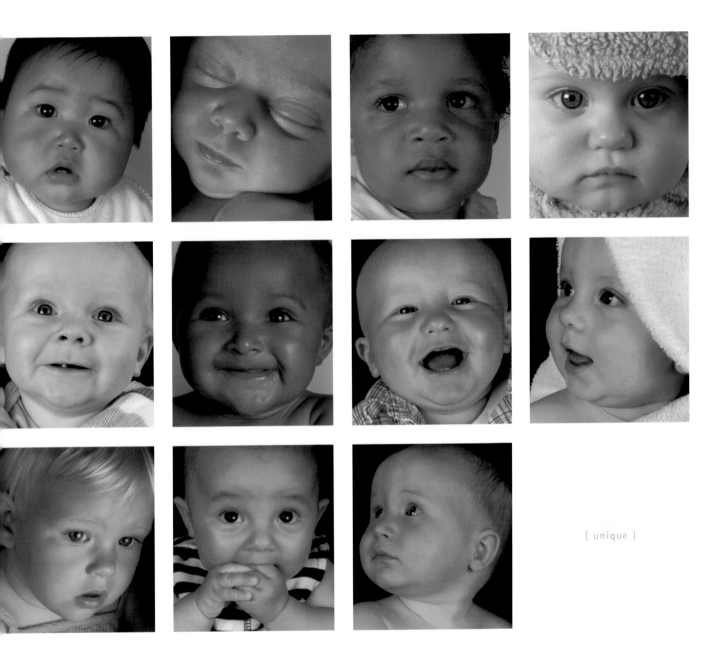

[unique]

a *chronicle* of your baby's early days

before

page 9

page 25

page 33

w e l c

f a m

g r

s h

o m page 15 e

i l y

o w

a r page 41 e

m o m page 48 e n t s

keepsake

[our first sonogram]

It's lovely, but very strange.
I feel an incredible sense of intimacy
with my baby. I have already bonded with him—
or her—even though we haven't met yet.

Sarah Price | Mother-to-be

b e f o r e

The birth of a baby is a beginning. It is the start of a

journey, not only for your little one but also for you, as

[anticipation]

you embark on parenthood and life as a family. This

precious time is all too brief, passing by in a blur of milestones and kisses.

Make your own memento of these special and unique moments by adding your

thoughts, feelings, and photos [   ] to this journal, to look back on with your

family as it grows and expands.

waiting for you . . .

due date

sonogram date(s)

10   The future is not something we enter.

The future is something we create.

Leonard Sweet | Author & theologian

names for a boy

names for a girl

cravings

[bump!]

I loved my bump!

Every kick and movement was a reminder

of the precious miracle

growing inside me.

Emily Howe | New mother

12

A new baby is like the beginning of all things —

wonder, hope, a dream of possibilities.

Eda Le Shan | Educator & author

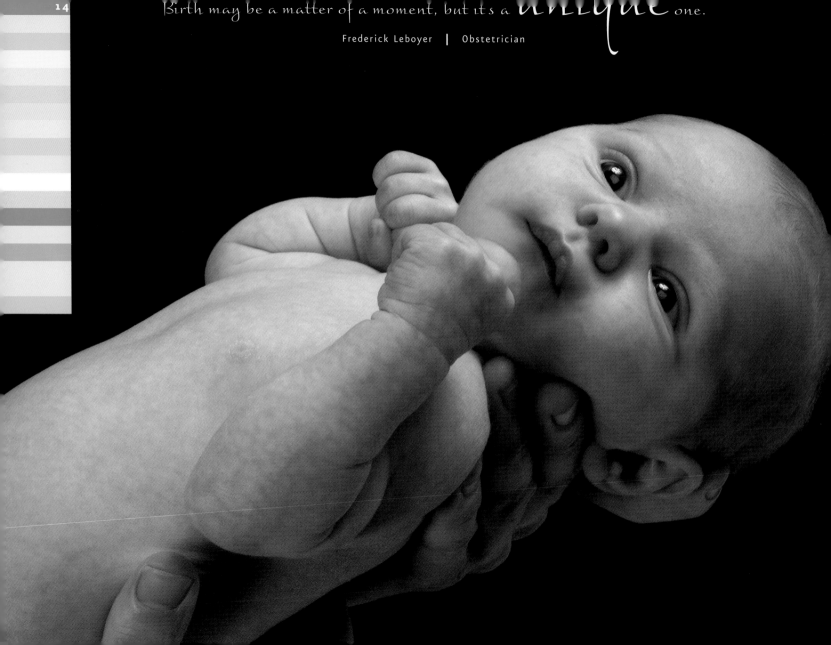

Birth may be a matter of a moment, but its a *unique* one.

Frederick Leboyer | Obstetrician

welcome

lily | purity

[the big day]

When you were born, you cried
and the world rejoiced.

Native American proverb

[beautiful]

Babies are such a nice way to start people.

Don Herold | Author

birth . . .

18

As soon as my baby was born, I couldn't remember what my old life was like. The day before felt like a million years ago.   Lisa Davies | Mother keepsake

The little plastic name tag conjures memories of my fragile newborn. Is it possible she was once so tiny?

Hannah Graham | Mother

Lucky the woman who knows the pangs of birth,

for she has held a star. Larry Barretto | Author

hello, baby . . .

your . . .

name

birthday

time of birth

place of birth

weight

length

head circumference

eye color

hair color

star sign

first visitors

Sometimes the smallest things are

the most important things.

Nigel Longuet | Father

early days . . .

22

We can do no great things, only

small things with great love.

Mother Teresa

The most precious moments of my life

were those I spent rocking, cuddling,

and singing lullabies to my child.

Krystyna Bublick | Author

[all smile]

The family is one of nature's masterpieces.

George Santayana | Philosopher & poet

[and baby makes three!]

Call it a clan, call it a network, call it a tribe, call it a

f a m i l y

— whatever you call it, whoever you are, you need one.

Jane Howard | Author

thoughts . . .

[delighted]

26

mom . . .

name

date of birth

place of birth

job

star sign

eye color

hair color

when I met your daddy

thoughts when you were born

dad . . .

[proud]

thoughts . . .

name

date of birth

place of birth

job

star sign

eye color

hair color

when I met your mommy

thoughts when you were born

You are going to know this person better

than you will ever know anybody else.

Penelope Leach | Child psychologist & author

our family . . .

28

Family faces are magic mirrors. Looking at people
who belong to us, we see the past, present,
and future. Gail Lumet Buckley | Author

[loving]

[kind]

[warm]

[gentle]

sharing . . .

29

[special]

[excited]

[thrilled]

[important]

celebrate . . .

[wise]

[understanding]

[fun]

[caring]

Other things may change us, but we **start** and end with the family.

Anthony Brandt | Author & journalist

The **best** things you can give children,
next to good habits, are good memories.

Sydney J. Harris | Author & journalist

grow

[baby's first year]

milestones . . .

34

All babies follow the same path of physical development but each one goes down that path at her own particular rate.

Penelope Leach | Child psychologist

first . . .

outing

smile

tooth

laugh

rolled over

clapped hands

animal noise

word

crawled

"cruised"

walked

[cute]

3 months . . .

grow . . .

length

weight

head circumference

35

favorite . . .

places

toys

songs

likes

dislikes

[inquisitive]

6 months . . .

grow . . .

length

weight

head circumference

favorite . . .

toys

food

places

songs

likes

dislikes

[gorgeous]

9 months . . .

_____

_____

_____

_____

_____

_____

_____

_____

_____

grow . . .

_____
length

_____
weight

_____
head circumference

37

favorite . . .

_____
toys

_____

_____
food

_____

_____
places

_____

_____
songs

_____

_____
likes

_____

_____
dislikes

_____

12 months . . .

38

If you can give your son or daughter
only one gift, let it be enthusiasm.

Bruce Barton | Author & advertising executive

[on the move]

grow . . .

height

weight

early words

likes

dislikes

first birthday . . .

gifts

party

[happy birthday!]

How far that little candle throws his beams!

William Shakespeare

share

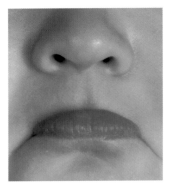 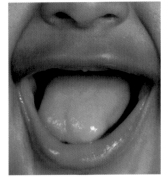

[thoughts and feelings]

precious memories . . .

4 2

You have a lifetime to work, but
children are only young once.

Polish proverb

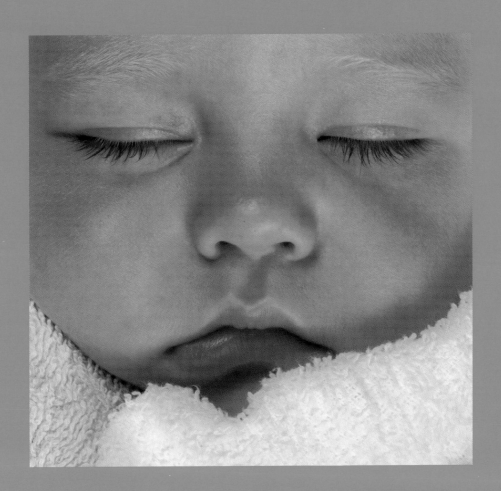

Always kiss your children goodnight,
even if they are already asleep.

H. Jackson Brown Jr. | Author

hopes and dreams . . .

44

When I approach a child, he inspires in me
two sentiments: tenderness for what he is,
and respect for what he may become.

Louis Pasteur

A child's world is fresh and new and beautiful,

full of wonder and excitement.   Rachel Carson | Author

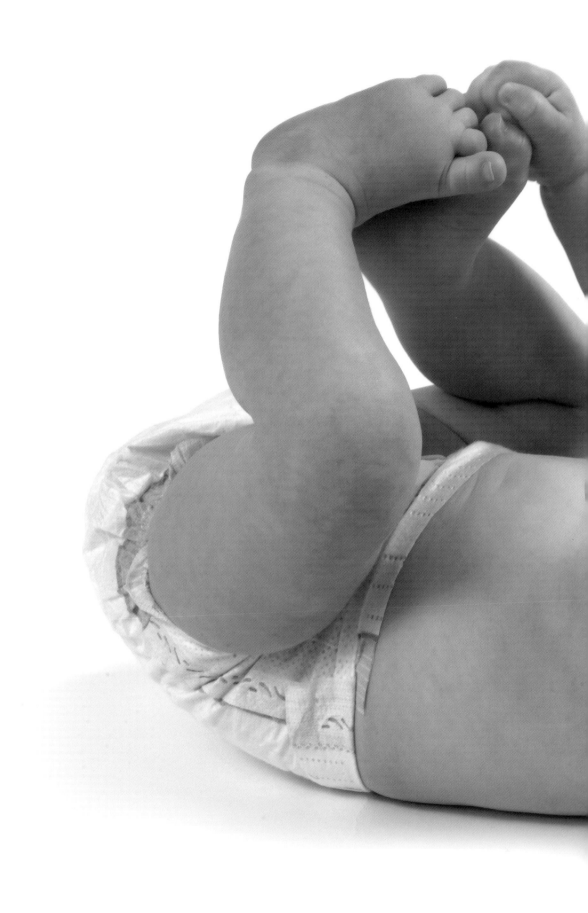

While we try to teach our children all about life,
our children teach us what life is all about.

Angela Schwindt | Author

[precious]

daffodil | *joy*

m o m e n t s

[play]

We do not remember days; we remember moments.

Cesare Pavese | Author

[curious]

50

2 years . . .

grow . . .

height

weight

birthday gifts

likes

dislikes

precious moments

[creative]

3 years . . .

grow . . .

height

weight

birthday gifts

likes

dislikes

precious moments

[wonderful]

5²

grow . . .

4 years . . .

height

weight

birthday gifts

likes

dislikes

precious moments

funniest moments

[clever]

5 years . . .

Before you know it, the toy is replaced by a schoolbag,
and the bashful smile by a confident grin.

Edie Sawle | Mother

wow!

height

weight

birthday gifts

53

likes

dislikes

wants to be

achievements

precious moments

The world tips away when we *look* into our children's faces.

Louise Erdrich | Author

[pensive]

54

[shy]

[happy]

[precious]

[mischievous]

[lively]

[sleepy]

[unique!]

The child must know that he is a miracle,
that since the beginning of the world there hasn't been,
and until the end of the world there will not be, another child like him.

Pablo Casals | Cellist and conductor

Use this page to record your baby's handprints.

12 months